HAIKU
RHAPSODIES

(Verses from Ghana)

Celestine Nudanu

ISBN: 978-9988-2-3286-3

THOUGHTS ABOUT HAIKU RHAPSODIES

Celestine Nudanu's *Haiku Rhapsodies* is an exhilarating collection of haiku for lovers of poetry. The author succeeds in transporting the reader into her world by creating very animated and serene scenes as she explores themes such as nature, death and love. The skill of the haiku poet is brevity and this is Celestine's forte, using few words which like magic are enchanting.

The reader cannot help but ask for more.

Vera Doku – Publisher, Readme Magazine

As an educator, I've been reminded of how little value our populace places on the Arts. A pity really, when you consider that the Arts - writing, music, drama, art and other new arts like graphics, has the ability to heal us. Generations of children are growing up without knowing how to reach that innermost part of the soul with expressions of song and dance.

With her love of words and the conveying of emotion, Celestine has allowed us to heal, opening up vistas of feeling that positively assault our senses.

carnival
masquerades display
autumn

So many colours envisioned that for a moment, my eyes could not handle it. From the soft sounds portrayed in:

garden path
the winds create
a crunch carpet

Celestine has that incredible ability to make you hear colours, see sounds and feel words. And those words aren't always warm and fuzzy. Take for example:

dark skies
the flap of wings
in a death dance

in which Celestine is able to use her words to evoke images of darkness, enough to give you goosebumps. For those of us who are visual learners, one can imagine a dark night, perhaps bats flying around and the cackle of a hyena in the distant gloom! Back and forth she takes us, from fast paced dances to slower paced mementos of *The Divine*.

Haiku My Heart should be everyone's Valentine! Short and Sweet, as Ghanaians love to say, enough to send the message:

butter on toast
the taste of you
at breakfast

For those who have forgotten the simple pleasure of being in love, *Haiku My Heart* will take you right through the gamut of emotions that love brings!

Haiku seem easy to write but they are definitely not. Celestine has honed this skill and now presents us with memorable verses that show us that less can definitely be more and we are blessed.

Congratulations!

Dr. Mary Asabea Ashun,
Deputy Principal, GIS; Author, Mistress of the Game and
Tuesday's Child

Haiku Rhapsodies delivers just as it promises; a collection of exquisite three-lined poems written from the heart, with a lyrical flair underlying the brevity that this collection of haiku has mastered.

With the various themes explored in the anthology, Celestine draws the reader into the complex yet fascinating phenomena of what life is all about - *Love, Death, Life* itself and the *Divine*. The beauty is that Celestine does so with panache and in so few words.

Haiku Rhapsodies will lift you to ecstatic levels and leave you positively giddy.

Unputdownable!

Nana Awere Damoah,
Author, Sebitically Speaking and I Speak of Ghana

Haiku as a genre is rather unknown on the Ghanaian literary landscape. It is testimony to Celestine's uncommon appetite that she has discovered this poignant literary form and has proceeded to espouse it with admirable fervour.

Fruit of a free and fresh imagination, yet steeped in the tradition of the mastery of the capture of intense thought through prose, this collection is an authoritative kaleidoscope of everything and every emotion African.

Though beguilingly simple, it is a sodden tapestry of Celestine Nudanu's
cosmos.

Indulge, at the level of your choosing.

Kasise Ricky Peprah
Founder, Youth Enterprise Development Network
Blogger, the Intelligent Ramblings of the Forgotten Seer

Celestine Nudanu's *Haiku Rhapsodies (Verses from Ghana)* is an exquisitely delightful collection, transcending the present time and space.

I have been transported through the different seasons, summer, winter, spring and fall, all in in one breath; The intensity of love and pain, jump out of the pages, tagging along and leaving one with very palpable emotions.

The verses on *the Divine,* so explicitly and expertly arranged presents God in an enchanting way, leaving one awestruck; it is refreshing to encounter God in such a simple yet very potent way.

The *Afriku* verses, varying in colour and taste, present a rich and yet delicate balance with strong sights and sounds; these ting out loudly, even in a quiet room.

Excellent work! Expertly arranged! A must read for all.

Mrs. Mary Abena Agyepong
Consultant, Higher Education Management

With *Haiku Rhapsodies,* Celestine has delivered a wonderful book full of gems. A few years ago I met Celestine online at Carpe Diem Haiku Kai, my daily haiku meme. Then she was just a novice in haiku. During the years she improved her haiku writing skills and I have seen her grow... and now... with this haiku anthology she dives into the 'big world'.

With this anthology she has reached a milestone ... I am glad and proud that she has made this anthology after several years of publishing and sharing her beautiful haiku at *Carpe Diem Haiku Kai.*

As I read *Haiku Rhapsodies,* I was overwhelmed by the beauty of her haiku and I love to bring a few haiku in the spotlight:

empty calabash
reflects the fading sun
a beggar sits in gloom

This haiku describes a scene, which is seen very often, but it's not the fading sun here but the beggar who has the lead. It is a haiku in which I easily can recognize the spirit of Basho. (one of the four greatest haiku poets ever)

Another nice haiku, a masterpiece in my opinion:

morning dew
on yellow buds
blooming dandelions

Well ... what can I say more? This haiku reflects the quality of Celestine's *Haiku Rhapsodies.*

Enjoy the read.

Chèvrefeuille (penname of Kristjaan Panneman)
Owner and Host of Carpe Diem Haiku Kai, a daily haiku meme.
Netherlands

Poetry is essential to my life. I love everything about the genre. Well, almost everything. I've found the haiku form daunting, uninviting, and unwelcoming. I can't explain it but my attitude towards haiku has been visceral; until Celestine Nudanu started blogging about haiku. Because she is a dear friend and because I like her writing, I started to read her poems - these haiku published here. And then I found there was much to appreciate, much to love about haiku.

Celestine's poems are light and heavy all at once. They are imbued with details of our Ghanaian life, the colours of our childhood, the blooms on the trees we played under, the laughter of an era of hardship that as kids we skipped, jumped and laughed through.

For me, Celestine's haiku have evoked nostalgia and made me mindful, thankful also of life now. Perhaps, this was the prescription for my haiku-aversion all along. I needed a poet to bring it home to me. And Celestine is that poet.

Enjoy the read.

Kinna Likimani
Mbaasem Foundation, Blogger at Kinna Reads (www.kinnareads.
com)

DEDICATION

I dedicate this book to the glory of God, my Alpha and Omega.

And also to the memory of my father, Nana Kwadwo Peprah Siase, (Anthony Peprah) Mansehene of Wamfie.

To my mother, Madam Patience Agbenu, for her love and sacrifices over the years. Thank you Sister.

And to the growth of haiku in Ghana.

EXPRESSION OF GRATITUDE

I'm grateful to the following persons for the various roles they played to bring this anthology to fruition;

- My husband, Gameli for his support

- My kids, Cedric, Cyril and Cecil for the good cheer

- Kristjaan Paneman, Netherlands and of *CDHK*. You taught me the fine art of haiku.

- Alice Keys, USA, and also of *Haiku Horizon*. Your weekly haiku meme is a great inspiration.

- Rebecca of *Recuerda Mi Corazon*, USA, for the weekly meeting of wonderful souls bent on sharing love, even on the blogosphere.

- Gilly, UK, for the *Lazy Poet's Thursday Haiku;* those lovely photos that inspired me to write.

- Vera Akumiah, for your belief in me.

- Adjei Agyei Baah, *(AHN)*, for your strong support and belief in me. You are truly a brother.

- Hamish Gunn. What can I say? Your forest is my forest, right here in Ghana!

- Comfort Pappoe, for this work and your patience.

- Belinda Bobbie, for your support.

- Dr. Mawuli Adzei, for your invaluable support

- And to all my wonderful friends, both here and on the blogosphere, who have inspired me over the years.

Thank You

CONTENTS

Thoughts About Haiku Rhapsodies
Dedication
Expression of Gratitude
Forward

Themes

FORWARD

A novice may ask "what is haiku"? Haiku in its simplest definition is a Japanese poem of mostly three lines that records a delightful moment in nature. According to Kaeru, it is a short poetry form written on a grain of rice. This definition posits the brevity and compactness of this genre. But though quite short, there lies a moment of 'aha' which leaves a lasting impression on the mind of the reader.

Celestine's collection is a historic one which explores a field where no Ghanaian poet has ever published in hard print. Hence her work distinguishes her as a trailblazer among her contemporaries like *Nana Fredua-Agyeman, Jacob Kobina Ayiah Mensah, Prince K. Mensah* and other budding poets.

Indeed my encounter with Celestine started on a delightful note. It all happened at the last Ghana Poetry Festival, 2014 which I could not personally attend due to urgent family business. Being an enthusiast and devotee of haiku, my friends reported back to me that a lady came to read haiku at the event instead of the usual spoken word and poetry that audience were annually treated to. My curiosity piqued and I decided to search for her till we eventually met face-to-face at her office in Accra.

I simply fell in love with her humility and pieces. An old hand at the poetry genre, and an avid blogger, Celestine is modest about her achievements. Not wanting to draw much attention to herself or be in the limelight, her participation in world haiku contests is few and far between. I find that rather endearing.

I was also compelled to explore her blog *Reading Pleasure* and was amazed at some of her marvellous collection of haiku and other micro poetry forms which she has archived over the years.

I must say Celestine is a versatile poetess who writes haiku in her own way to reflect both her immediate African setting and foreign lands. Her collection is a fine blend of both local and universal themes which beautifully shed light on many cultures. She records with honesty through her power of observation, while being careful not to be lured into fleeting imagination which characterizes most modern haiku poets of today.

Among her lionized pieces which jumped at me and will remain my favourites are:

fireside
kids chatter
fills mother's cooking pot

lantern soot
wiping my memory
of you

In the campaign of many schools/poets to make haiku appear on UNESCO's list as one of the world's Intangible Heritage, it is Celestine's wish that her collection in this new field will inspire her peers and other up- coming poets to appreciate haiku and help Ghana find its rightful place on the world haiku map.

As a lover and promoter of haiku, I will recommend her collection for your past-time and also as a great present for friends and loved ones.

—*Adjei Agyei-Baah,*
Co-founder, Africa Haiku Network/ Co-founder, Poetry Foundation
Ghana. Co-editor, The Mamba.

Poetry cannot be caged like a bird - it must unfold its wings and fly

Roxi St. Clair

'Language is like an embryo. As letters slowly develop words turn to verse and then gasps...like an infant's first breath of air, poetry is born'

Roxi St. Clair

AFRIKU

Afriku are haiku of African origin, focusing on her rich images, rhythms, and unique settings peculiar to the culture and heritage of Africa.

Afriku in its simplest forms, also capture thrilling African moments in nature giving the reader an *aha* moment.

bamboo flute
rushing stream calms
the savannah

rugged footpath
the weight of the sun
in the mangoes

new day
a cockcrow stirs
the leaves

warm night
discarded clothes
and the feast of mosquitoes

black night
the voodoo priest shivers
at the moon

harmattan winds
coffee aroma
my companion

rustling silk
the sound of leaves
in harmattan

windless night
the full moon in my
barrel

mirage
the cocoyam leaf
shimmers

morning perfume
the valley's drums
rouse the lilies

farmland
sun-filled mangoes
track my steps

moonless night
an old lantern
dispels the shadows

fading sun
shadows the beggar's bowl
empty

empty calabash
reflects the fading sun
a beggar sits in gloom

talisman
scented oils
haunt the night

by the hearth
a cold breeze sways
her loin cloth

market day
the stench of unsold wares
fills her stomach

sundown
a mother gathers
her unsold melons

rumbling stomach
counting melons
at twilight

talking drums
the crow and the chick
in a war dance

red eyes
squeezing juice from stones
refugee kids

grinding stone
her ebony hue fades
in pepper soup

unsold fish
a mother's reflection
darkens the lagoon

smoky evening
love brews in African pot
my mother's meals

fireside
kids' chatter
fills mother's cooking pot

in tandem
child's thumping feet
and fufu pestle

noon heat
scent of fresh palm-wine
lingering

sound of water
the canoe drinks up
the lagoon

dark skies
the cry of the chick
in the mouth of a crow

moonless night
. rushing stream swallows
my paddle .

rush hour
hawkers trail the cars
bumper to bumper

prelude to harmattan
dust and rain
vie for attention

leafless tree
all that remains of
the harmattan

advancing army
bound with a single sash
just brooms

ancient paths
stench of decay sweeps
his footsteps

midday nap
a string of beads
her only cover

lantern soot
wiping my memory
of you

still in the
taste of medicine
grandma's chicken soup

noon heat
a lizard basks in
yesterday's raindrops

silent ripples
a splinter of the moon
in my barrel

how long
to wait for your return
the mangoes bloom

Carmelopardalis
romancing the stars
from far away savannahs

NATURE

One of haiku's main appeal is that it focuses on nature or aspects of it. Haiku, in its brevity, capture that special moments in time when all our senses are alight to the wonders and beauty of nature; that *aha* moment when the 'nickel drops', and we are in tune with nature.

On the other hand, the *Senryu* while not focusing on nature per se, highlight aspects of human nature with a twist of humour.

All these verses create an opening through which we can feed our minds and souls and end up cleansed.

twilight
creeping shadows cover
my wrinkles

sky party
after the rains
the rainbow

carnival
masquerades display
autumn

morning dew
on yellow buds
blooming dandelions

garden path
dry winds create
a crunch carpet

endless skies
ribbon of colours splits
into a rainbow

evening walk
passing by the hedges
a shimmer of colours

tree top
hidden from view
the nest of a wandering cuckoo

reflection
my mother stares
back at me

moonless night
suddenly the forest is ablaze
with fireflies

across the skies
sudden expanse of sheath
migrating swallows

silent splinter
through the darkness
a halo

the night
in flames
fireflies

blue moon
the forest weaves its charm
on me

dawn chorus
birdsong drowns out
the muezzin's call

sundown
faint shadows cover
my nakedness

bedroom talk
scent of cherry blossoms
fills the gap

raindrops
just a drop
the basil blooms

through the mist
silver rays kiss the leaves
the dew, the dew

ah, the light
spring's shimmer
in the river

two stars
remnants of the
full moon's banquet

sunset
i catch the glow between
my fingers

at break of dawn
in place of the full moon
two twinkling stars

snaking stream
sun shadows
the damselfly

endless kiss
the horizon and meadows
are one

tidal waves
a pebble
in the fisherman's net

rippling puddle
a frog takes a dip
amidst the algae

sudden rain
my long face
scuttles for shelter

light rain
the scent of dandelions
budding in the palm

fireflies
the kids render the darkness
useless

dark skies
the flap of wings
in a death dance

stunts
the lure of mountains and oceans
batman forever

billowing waves
crashing against
empty shells

ripples
the stream silently eats up
the rocks

swaying leaves
the sound of silence
at dawn

echoes
the wind intrudes
in my dreams

sleepless night
I blink
with the stars

looking closely
into the darkness
glint of silver web

beach fever
summer rays sheath
my nudity

spilled coffee
the moon's reflection
in a pool

ecstasy
waterfalls caressing
summer heat

scented breath
waiting to inhale
April

fresh breeze
another life in the
cuckoo's nest

these violets
keep reaching for the skies
summer baptism

summer twilight
the melody of mating
cicadas

almost as one
scent of opening buds
fill my emptiness

morning thrill
petals open up to
the dew

waterfalls
not even the stars can
dim all that sparkle

aqua fresh
verdant rocks
in silver

under the willow
hiding from glare of the sun
lovers' stolen kiss

moon drizzle
prelude to the
morning's splinter

a long trek
up ancient roads
scent of honeysuckles

midnight rains
my roof drums
a lullaby

full steam
scent of coffee lingering
after the rain

even beautiful
a shimmer of dry leaves
littering the grounds

swirling clouds
my tea cup fills with
shadows

HAIKU
MY HEART

Verses written from the heart, just that. Based on observations of human nature, nature, family, romantic love and yes, well just a bit of the imagination.

They follow no pattern; just the brevity of the words, speaking from the heart to you. And often as is the case, what comes from the heart has a ring of truth in it.

mother's pride
his bead earrings
adorn me
(for Cyril)

these words
waltzing on paper
poetry with style

drawing my strength
from the morning breeze
andante andante

haunt my waking thoughts
with your luminous branding
for dusk cometh soon

sunshine
amidst the drizzle
fickle clouds

murky skies
searching for the light
in my darkness

rendezvous
the moon follows
our footsteps

dusk
walking by the bush
a crushed flower

wanton delight
the taste of mangoes
on my fingers

butter on toast
the taste of you
at breakfast

chocolate delight
Valentine's day
on my tongue

body fever
rising
ah, summer love song

night fever
song of the siren
rising

lone flower
I hide from my
mirror mirage

drizzle
a flower gasps
for just a drop

silhouette
our dance steps
on the moon

perfect tempo
losing myself in
your waves

rendezvous
a shadow falls into
another

champagne and you
on a moonlit night
the leaves sigh

gondola ride
together we rock
the waves

breezy night
a whiff of lavender in
her slumber

night pleasures
the feel of my bed
after a shower

just a touch
he lights my candle
with his breath

morning kiss
petals unfold to the
dewy touch

sun-kissed meadow
the stars come down
just for us

stolen moments
his words gather dust
on my ring

windy night
my name on his lips
faintly

night of words
I sip your musk
with my coffee

garden hues
the sexy taste
of my chilli

sleepless night
I cradle
your cologne

reckless night
the moon
goes pale

insomnia
the stars and I wink
at each other

breathless
just that look
and time suspends

summer heat
melting on our tongues
strawberries

behind the cafe
wandering fingers stroke
the hot night

starry night
I sheath my nakedness
with the dust

silver drops
my body in beads
after the rain

sleepless night
I shiver beside
the wind

like a flower
I open up for you
read me

wild breeze
the origami folds
and unfolds

midnight kiss
scented letter unfolds
its secrets

waning roses
the scent of
valentine night

valentine night
the kiss of stale champagne
on my breath

thousand lights
I see stars
in your kisses

champagne bliss
breeze of roses assail
the sultry night

Valentine
hype, fun, sex or love
taste and see

between the sheets
the warm nuzzle of
my poodle

lonely night
the smell of coffee returns
to haunt me

roses
and Dom Perignon
yours forever

balancing act
the precarious road
of a crooked love

THE DIVINE

It's all about the greatness of God and our relationship with him, written with an enchanting and yet profound touch. Are we heaven bound?

These are more *Senryu* than *Haiku*, with a twist of humour.

heaven bound
the weight of our sins
squash the clouds

Jacob's ladder
the rungs groan
with sins

flute notes
God's breath stirs
the dawn

after the storm
in sprouting leaves
the chirp chirp of Noah's dove

where is God
reason flees in the spit of
machine fire

edge of skies
raindrops fall as tears
Easter prelude

raindrops
ticking off the days
to Easter

concerto
raindrops sing
Hosanna

rivulets
His blessings
on parched lands

empty tomb
above the echoes
Jesus lives

waking dream
heaven mocks
my sins

in anguish
my only refuge
is high up

a glimpse of heaven
through cotton clouds
the palm tree in supplication

washing my feet
I tread my master's path
cautiously

choir celestial
waves and waves
flood the earth

cloudy dawn
God's voice
in the medley of drizzle

child prodigy
banquet of fish and bread
to the rescue

ultimate test
in place of the lamb
a ram

Sunday afternoon
tracing the path of angels
with my breath

dark night
coat of many colours
lights the way

divine rights
gold fish morphs
into men

the sound of my voice
above the clouds
gratitude

opium
healing the world
with the Word

birdsong
tweeting
the goodness of God

on the mountaintop
breathing in the skies
and His presence

first snow
the relief of pilgrims
at the melting manna

DEATH

The leveller! Is it to be feared, craved or welcomed?

I dare say that these verses capture that final moment of our lives in a poignant way, the *'ahaness'* giving it an almost beauty that only haiku can give.

moaning all night
the palm tree bows in
silent farewell

dark clouds
billowing curtains
close his days

fresh lilies
the little girl's gift
sways the casket

stained window
the morning mist evaporates
silently

freezing cold
the warm breath
of dying love

sundown
his last words illuminate
my freedom

last breath
the Oak sheds its leaves
in sleep

bedside vigil
his breath fades with
my memories

dying flame
I exhale your shadow through
the times

dreaming of the stars
you forgot to say goodbye
that final journey

lingering fragrance
mother's scarf
frayed with memories

He Is Risen

between death
and resurrection
the veil peels
and darkness
fades to a gossamer thin
revealing the glow
of immortal bloom
his shroud a blossom in Spring
the tomb His victor
then hush, bleeding piece of dust
we rise, for He is risen.

What Is Man

what is man
that walks on all fours
we are flies

a light swat
then we are no more
puffing wind

to live or to die
as wanton boys to mango
we're squashed with a breath
so I am no less than me
and you are no less than you

For Kofi Awonoor

winds of death
sweep in a convulsing arc
we strive for meaning

we strive for meaning
in a world of blood and tears
frozen in our hearts

frozen in our hearts
grief blurs with unspoken words
nation mourns her son

nations mourns her son
as Africa kills her sun
we strive for meaning

CONNECT WITH THE AUTHOR

Twitter: http://twitter.com/cestone40
Facebook: https://facebook.com/haikurhapsodies/
Facebook: http://facebook.com/cnudanu
Blog: readinpleasure.wordpress.com
Email: cestone40@hotmail.com